WE WENT TO THE ZOO TODAY
THE GOLDEN AGE OF ZOO POSTCARDS

26. 8. 02

Dear Sir,

I beg to
confirm my cable
as follows

"Adult perfect"
"Skeleton nigerian"
"Hippopotamus"
"35 pounds reply"
"from Cross"

Yours Truly S. Cross

We went to the zoo today...

The Golden Age of Zoo Postcards

By Alan Ashby

Published by the Independent Zoo Enthusiasts Society

DEDICATED TO THE MEMORY OF MICHAEL ASHBY (1949 - 2006)

Copyright ©Alan Ashby, 2009
ISBN 978-0-9563831-0-5
Published by the Independent Zoo Enthusiasts Society
PO Box 4, Todmorden, Lancs OL14 6DA
www.izes.co.uk

Text and design by Alan Ashby
Sub-edited by Loveday Cuming
Printed by Advent Colour, Andover, Hants SP10 3LU

Front cover: Asian elephant 'Dr Jim' at London Zoo, postmarked 1906. Back cover: Chimpanzee 'Kruger' and his keeper at Bristol Zoo, early 1900s; Camel Ride at London Zoo, postmarked 1905; 'Riding the 200-year-old Tortoise. The Zoo, London', postmarked 1927.

ACKNOWLEDGEMENTS
I would like to thank the owners of the cards used in this book: Tim Brown, Jim Clubb, Brian Foster, Tim May, Ross Meredith, Paul Murphy, Rob Vaughan and Ron Willis. I would also like to thank John Adams, Loveday Cuming, John Edwards, Karyn Sparks and Jeremy Speed for their help and encouragement. A full bibliography would be far too long to include, but I would like to acknowledge all the authors who have contributed to the Bartlett Society Journals and the late Clinton Keeling in particular, who founded the Bartlett Society (zoohistory.co.uk) and self-published many very helpful books.

Contents

"I'LL DO YOU"

RHESUS MONKEY – DUDLEY ZOO.

Foreword

It is said that there is a museum for almost everything in the UK... yet despite an ongoing, even increasing, popularity, no museum exists for zoos. The contribution of zoos to popular culture has been enormous, making stars of individual animals such as 'Chi Chi' or 'Jumbo', or giving countless millions a glimpse of the earth's biodiversity.

Today's zoos are forward-thinking establishments looking to create a seamless interaction with the conservation of fauna (and even some flora) in the wild – without a doubt they are a little bashful, even afraid, of their past. Maybe that is the reason why zoo history is underserved and it is almost certainly the reason why there is no zoo museum.

We Went To The Zoo Today... does not celebrate the past with its iron bars and, occasionally, lack of empathy with captive animals, but it gives an important glimpse, via postcards, of the attitudes of days gone by. It took a long time for photographs of animals, either in zoos or the wild, to appear commonly in print; the first known photograph taken in a zoo appeared in 1851, and fifty years were to elapse before the medium proliferated.

Postcards became the main arena in which zoos, their architecture and animals, also employees and visitors, were photographed prior to the First World War, so their historical importance cannot be understated.

Alan Ashby is totally correct to identify this significance and place it in the context of a book. A number of different aspects of yesterday's zoos are represented; they were times when there was no concern over obtaining animals from any part of the globe and no import restrictions, but at the same time many of today's commonly seen species were rare, unknown or difficult to keep alive. Captive breeding was an incidental achievement, not a necessity. The thylacine (page 33), for example, was known to be rare but no one thought to try and remedy this situation by breeding it in zoos. It is, of course, now an extinct species.

The subject of zoos is a multidisciplinary one, and its history involves people just as much as animals. Architecture, fashion, social values, education and so on – if all animal life wasn't at the zoo, much of human life often was. *We Went To The Zoo Today...* offers an illuminating pictorial insight into our species going about one of its favourite activities over a half-century period. And perhaps in that statement lies the ultimate significance of the zoo historian and the reason why there should be a zoo museum.

Tim Brown,
Chairman,
Independent Zoo Enthusiasts Society,
Todmorden, Lancashire.

The History of the Picture Postcard

As with the introduction of many innovations, cost was an important factor in the invention of the postcard. The idea was to provide a cheaper means of communication, and postcards were lighter and more easily handled than letters; more importantly, due to their standard size, they could be sent at a lower postal rate.

They originated on the continent but by 1870 had arrived in Britain as plain cards – message on one side, address on the other. They could only be issued by the Post Office with a pre-printed 'stamp'. Although a limited number of these cards were illustrated it was usually with advertisements, and they didn't really catch the imagination of the British public.

It wasn't until 1894 that the Post Office relinquished its monopoly and allowed other parties to produce cards for use with a halfpenny adhesive stamp as proof that postage had been paid. The picture postcard had arrived.

However, the Post Office still insisted that one side only be used for the address alone. The problem was, how much space should be taken up by the picture and how much by the message? Because of this, picture postcards did not immediately become a big success.

The major change that allowed the introduction of picture postcards as we still know them today came about in 1902, when the Post Office allowed the use of the 'divided back' – a British innovation. Both the address and the message could be confined to one side – message on the left, address on the right – which left the other side completely free for any type of illustration the publisher wanted to use. In September of that year, a printed

Between 1894 and 1902, only postcards with the picture and the message both on the same side were allowed by the Post Office.

CHESSINGTON ZOO. ZEBRA AND FOAL

PAIGNTON ZOO. ZEBRA AND FOAL

Grevy's zebra and foal at London Zoo. Both of these cards are incorrectly captioned.

line was introduced that clearly divided the two sides of the card.

From then on, postcards exploded in popularity, and quickly became the standard medium for transmitting short messages. As the email of those times, they were cheap and reliable, with up to seven postal deliveries a day. People also bought them in great numbers to keep as souvenirs, which explains why so many of the earliest examples are unposted. Also the postcard itself often became the reason for its use – 'one for your collection' is often a part of the sender's message.

Picture postcards and zoos were ideally suited to one another. Collections of exotic animals have been popular for hundreds of years. In the UK, static and travelling menageries, where the public paid to see exotic beasts assembled from the far corners of the earth, date back to the early 18th century (private collections of exotic animals, usually owned by nobility, date back even further than this).

The word 'zoo' was an abbreviation that came into popular use during the 1840s. By the end of the 19th century, zoos were well established: the UK had seen at least two dozen open to the public, and it is generally accepted that the 'golden age' of postcards was between 1902 and 1914 – the outbreak of the First World War. During this time, since there was of course no colour photography, many cards were hand-tinted. The colouring would be left to the imagination of the artists, since they did not have the view nor animal subject itself to observe, and the quality and accuracy of their renditions vary enormously. Furthermore, two identical photographs might be painted quite differently by different artists. A relaxed attitude to exactly when and where the photograph was first taken was also not unknown. For instance, the two identical cards

shown on the page opposite, both probably produced in the 1930s, show a zebra with her foal at London Zoo – not Chessington or Paignton – photographed in 1927, which was before Chessington had even opened!

These and other anomalies make collecting postcards a fascinating hobby and a never-ending source of pleasure. While compiling this book, I have found myself drawn into not only a hundred-plus years of zoo history, but also into the intimate and often touching world of the postcard senders and recipients.

Alan Ashby

POSTCARD CHRONOLOGY

c.1869. First postcard is posted in Austria.

1870. Postcards first introduced into Britain.

1894. Pictures introduced by independent publishers.

1899. Standard size of 5.5in x 3.5in introduced.

1902. The 'divided back' first allowed by the Post Office.

THIS SPACE AS WELL AS THE BACK MAY BE USED FOR INLAND COMMUNICATION. POST-OFFICE REGULATION.

Postage stamps. When the postmark is indistinct, the stamp used can give an indication as to when a card was posted.

1900 - 1901	1902 - 1904	1904 - 1910	1911 - 1912	1912 - 1918	1918 - 1921	1921 - 1922
HALFPENNY	HALFPENNY	HALFPENNY	HALFPENNY	HALFPENNY	ONE PENNY	THREE HALFPENCE
VICTORIA	**EDWARD VII**	**EDWARD VII**	**GEORGE V**	**GEORGE V**	**GEORGE V**	**GEORGE V**

1922 - 1934	1934 - 1936	1936	1937 - 1940	1940 -1941	1941 - 1950	1950 - 1952
ONE PENNY	ONE PENNY	1D	1D	2D	2D	2D
GEORGE V	**GEORGE V**	**EDWARD VIII**	**GEORGE VI**	**GEORGE VI**	**GEORGE VI**	**GEORGE VI**

'A happy family at Wombwells', c.1900s. Static and travelling menageries pre-date zoos by more than one hundred years. During the heyday of picture postcards, wild-beast shows in one form or another were commonplace. When this photograph was taken, Bostock & Wombwell's operated the largest and most famous of the menageries. The man in the centre holding a young sloth bear is general manager Harold Birkett, who was married to Annie Bostock.

Biddales Menagerie, c.1900s. In the highly competitive atmosphere of the fairgrounds the Front, or 'Flash', was extremely important – the bigger the better. A carefully painted sign above the Biddales entrance reads, 'ORENZO enters the den with the untamable LION Sultan.' 'Lorenzo the lion tamer' had been a famous name for many years when this photograph was taken. A rival show – Sedgwick's Menagerie – also had a lion tamer known as 'Lorenzo'. Biddales has corrupted the famous name to confuse the public.

Bostock & Wombwell's Royal No. 1 Menagerie at Hull Fair, 1906. A young sloth bear was used to draw the crowds while a band played continually, either at the front or inside as part of the show. Hull was a major venue for many travelling menageries. The annual fair continues to this day, although the last time that Bostock & Wombwell visited was in October 1931.
The Zoological Society of London purchased most of the menagerie's animals in December of that year to augment the stock at its newly opened country zoo at Whipsnade in Bedfordshire.

Captain Purchase's Lions, c.1932. The two dancing girls are sisters Gracie (left) and Rosie Purchase. Rosie would dance in the lion's cage while her father, 'Captain' Tommy Purchase, who was in the cage with her, managed the lions. It was a prelude to his lion-taming act. Captain Purchase died in 1932, just a few weeks after being seriously mauled by a lion. In 1934, Rosie married Jimmy Chipperfield, the famous circus entrepeneur and inventor of the safari park concept.

"GOLIATH," the Wonder Sea Elephant.
Exhibited by Frank Bostock.   The first and only one in Gt. Britain.

"Lion Wallace" Purchases Menagerie.

''Goliath', the Wonder Sea Elephant. Exhibited by Frank Bostock. The first and only one in Gt. Britain', postmarked 1932. This animal was obtained from the German animal dealer Carl Hagenbeck. A special waterproof canvas tank was made to house him. It was possibly not the first elephant seal to arrive in Great Britain, as London Zoo had exhibited one in 1911 and Hagenbeck's elephant seals – the first to be seen alive in Europe – had arrived just a few months earlier in 1910.

Lion 'Wallace' at Purchases Menagerie, c.1910s. 'Wallace' was a popular name for lions. The original Wallace reputedly belonged to George Wombwell and achieved notoriety at an infamous 'lion fight' in Warwick. Wombwell advertised that he intended to set his lions against bull mastiffs. Wallace inflicted such appalling injuries on the dogs that the fight was abandoned.

Just as the name Wallace was used for many different lions, this photograph also appeared on other contemporary postcards. Day's Menagerie, for instance, used exactly the same image.

'Home breeding at Wombwells.' Lioness with cubs at Bostock & Wombwell's menagerie, c.1910s. Lions bred well in the travelling menageries which was surprising, as seclusion and quiet were not easily achieved.

Beast wagons were cleverly designed: the thick bar at the bottom unhooked to facilitate feeding – an idea copied by London Zoo – and the wire netting seen covering the bars on the right prevented the animal next door from reaching around.

Lion cubs in a menagerie, postmarked Scarborough, 20 August 1913. The back of this card is hardly legible but states, 'I went to two aquariums this afternoon with Teddy... saw these two dear little baby lions. They were not in a cage but with their keeper in the Hall. There were some lovely big lions too.' The writer then goes on to say, 'This morning we walked to the Mere...' Also mentioned is Filey, a small seaside resort just a few miles along the coast from Scarborough. The uniforms are typical of those worn by members of the Bostock & Wombwell troupe. An intriguing card.

Main Entrance, Zoological Gardens, London

Main Entrance to London Zoo, c.1909. The zoo was open from 9am until half an hour after sunset. The charge for admission in 1909 was one shilling (five pence) for adults and sixpence (two and a half pence) for children. However, on Mondays throughout the year and on certain days during the holiday season, the charge was sixpence for all. On Sundays the zoo was closed, except to Fellows of the Zoological Society of London and their friends, and to those provided with special tickets.

London : The Parrots at "The Zoo."

Parrots at London Zoo, postmarked 1910. At the time this photograph was taken, London Zoo probably had the finest collection of parrots in the world. This path is on the south bank of the Regent's Canal, and was adjacent to the Parrot House. The lady on the right has stepped over the low barrier and is happily risking a bite from a macaw's beak!

London "The Zoo" -- Monkey House

Monkey House at London Zoo, c.1902. This house was built in 1864 and demolished hurriedly in 1926 following an outbreak of tuberculosis among its occupants. It was built in a conservatory style with an iron and glass roof, and had no outdoor accommodation for its inhabitants. In 1900, author F.G. Aflalo wrote, 'This building in spite of its poor accommodation on full days, in spite of its dreadful atmosphere on all days, is among the first goals of those who pass the turnstiles.'

In the Monkey House.   The Zoo.

I will let you know how we get on tomorrow. Have you been lighting if it is fine we might go out Sunday last Sunday

Interior of the Monkey House at London Zoo, postmarked 1906. There were large central compartments in which 'individuals which could be got to agree' were kept together, and the walls were lined with small separate cages. Double doors kept out fresh air and it was over-heated by large water pipes, as seen in this card. By 1903, this house was considered to be unsuitable for its purpose.

London Zoo from the air, c.1921. The 1902 Ape House can be seen in the centre. This was partly incorporated into the present Reptile House, which was completed in 1927. To the left of the Ape House is the Summer Aviary, which had a tunnel provided with seats built into it. The guidebook of the time stated, 'The lover of birds will be repaid by sitting in the tunnel quietly, when he will be able to see the birds living a natural life.' To the right, the 1864 Monkey House and the Antelope House, which was completed in 1861, can also be clearly seen.

BIRDSEYE VIEW OF THE ZOO

LONDON, ZOOLOGICAL GARDENS, THE BROWN BEAR.

734 THE ZOO. (London). — The Elephant at Work. — LL.

The Bear Pole at London Zoo, c.1900s. One of the original exhibits at the zoo, the Bear Pit and its iconic pole (c.1828) disappeared at about the same time that the Mappin Terraces, with their improved bear accommodation, were constructed. It was said that, on Tuesdays, the bears could hardly be bothered to climb the pole for tid-bits, as they had been fed so much by the large crowds who came to the zoo on the cheaper, 'sixpence for all' Mondays.

Asian elephant 'Dr Jim' at London Zoo, c.1900s. Dr Jim arrived at the zoo in 1896 and was used as a riding animal for many years. In 1908, he attacked a keeper and was subsequently sold to Buenos Aires Zoo in Argentina. Tragically, however, he died during the sea voyage.

Asian elephant 'Dr Jim' at London Zoo, c.1905. On the right is the eastern end of the Terrace, which was demolished in 1919. The western end survived into the 1960s. This card could be used to form an interesting panorama if it were laid out to the left of the card at the bottom of page 26.

759 THE ZOO (London). — The Lawn. — LL. *May 27th*

London. "The Zoo".

Asian elephant 'Dr Jim' at London Zoo, 1900s. The eastern wing of the Antelope House is seen on the left. Dr Jim is heading south towards the Park Paddocks.

THE ZOO.—THE ELEPHANT WITH PASSENGERS.

African bull elephant 'Jingo' at London Zoo, postmarked 1904. Jingo arrived in July 1882. This photograph was taken at least a couple of years before the card was posted, because Jingo left London zoo in March 1903. His attendant is senior keeper C. Eyles.

"LOFTY" (Jan Van Albert) MOSS EMPIRES' GIANT.
The tallest man in the world, 9ft. 3½in. Visits the Zoo, England.

"Lofty' (Jan Van Albert) Moss Empires' Giant. The tallest man in the world, 9ft 3½in, visits the zoo, England.' London Zoo, c.1920s.** Lofty almost always appeared with his showbusiness partner 'Seppetoni' (seen here, but not captioned on the card). They were a popular duo in travelling shows and variety theatres during the 1920s and 1930s.

The Elephant Steps at London Zoo, postmarked 1907. This early photograph includes 'Jingo' (on the right) and an Asian elephant, probably 'Suffa Culli', who was withdrawn from riding duties in 1900. Visitors were warned that the elephants were accustomed to being fed by the public and would snatch paper bags or handbags with their trunks if they believed that they contained buns.

Flamingos at London Zoo, postmarked 1904. At the time this photograph was taken the natural pink of newly arrived flamingos always faded to white in captive conditions, due to a dietary deficiency. Ironically, the artist who hand-coloured this card has very nearly reinstated the correct amounts of pink to this small flock.

AT THE ZOO. A TEAM OF LLAMAS.

'At the Zoo. A Team of Llamas.' London Zoo, c.1923. It was about 1912 when keepers at London Zoo first hitched llamas to a small cart. Before then, children were given rides on the llamas themselves, but they were never thought to be suitable as saddle animals.

At the Zoo   A ride on the Ass

'A ride on the Ass' at London Zoo, c.1920s. This is a view looking east towards the Deer and Cattle House and Wader's Aviary. To the right, one of the Lion House outdoor cages can also be seen.

Interior of the Lion House at London Zoo, posted 30 August 1906. This house was completed in 1876 and demolished almost exactly one hundred years later. The interior had a range of fourteen cages along its north side. Each den had two inside compartments, or sleeping dens. At the back of the building were day rooms and sleeping rooms for the keepers. A bust of Sir Stamford Raffles, first President of the Zoological Society of London, can be seen above the arched doorway, centre-right of this card.

London.   30/8/06   The Zoo, In the Lion House.

Indian lions at London Zoo, c.1920s. Four large outdoor cages were added to the Lion House in 1877. Communication between the inner dens and the outdoor cages was by means of an inconvenient movable gangway on rails. Later, in 1906, a series of bridges were erected. Additional outdoor cages were added in 1924.

This subspecies of lion is now classified as critically endangered; only 300 or so exist in the wild.

1115. STUDIES AT THE ZOO. "JOHN DANIEL" THE GORILLA.

Gorilla 'John Daniel' at London Zoo, 1920.
John Daniel was privately owned by a couple who had bought him in the pet department of a large London store for £300 in December 1918. He was loaned to the zoo for just a few hours each day. Although they were highly desirable as exhibits, gorillas were difficult to keep alive in the conditions offered by zoos of the day; seven had already died prematurely at London between 1888 and 1908. John Daniel lived in a private home and enjoyed almost constant human companionship, but inevitably he grew too large and strong for this arrangement to continue. In March 1921, he was sold to the Ringling Brothers circus in the US, where he fell ill and died just a few weeks later. Ironically, in this photograph, John Daniel is temporarily housed in a lion's den.

YOUNG CHIMPANZEES AT TEA

'Young Chimpanzees at Tea.' London Zoo, 1932. Chimpanzees have been imported into Europe from Africa for centuries and were always highly valued as exhibition animals that could draw large crowds. At London Zoo, various disparate tricks taught to the chimps eventually became the 'Chimps' Tea Party', held every afternoon throughout the summer months for many years. They were eventually discontinued in 1972, when the Michael Sobell Pavilions for Apes and Monkeys was opened.

Monkey Hill at London Zoo, postmarked 1936. This enclosure was constructed during the winter of 1924-25. It was not a great success, due to the excessive fighting among the eighty hamadryas baboons that were installed. For a time, the solution was to keep only males – as shown here – but eventually even this plan was abandoned. By the time the Second World War had begun, there were no baboons on Monkey Hill, and it was demolished sometime around 1956.

Polar Bear Enclosure at London Zoo, postmarked 1906. This enclosure was originally constructed in 1844. It was roofed over in 1851 after a bear had succeeded in climbing out.

POLAR BEAR CAGE, AT THE ZOO, LONDON.

Hyenas' & Bears' Dens at London Zoo, c.1905. By the time this photograph was taken, this row of cages was considered obsolete. However, the area was not redeveloped until 1919, partly because the dens were wrongly thought to be the work of Decimus Burton, the zoo's first architect. The First World War subsequently caused further delay.

The Bears' Dens.

The Zoo.

The Camel House at London Zoo, posted 5 October 1910.
Grade II-listed and often touted as one of the oldest buildings in the zoo, the Camel House has been radically altered or rebuilt a number of times in its long history. Originally constructed in 1828, the clock turret was added in 1831. The whole structure was rebuilt in 1844 and again in 1898. It was bomb-damaged in 1940, and once again completely rebuilt in 1947.

760   THE ZOO (London). — The Camel House. — LL.

Camel Ride at London Zoo, postmarked 1905.
A considerable amount of time and energy was used to break in riding animals such as elephants and camels; on busy days, the amount of revenue raised – twopence a ride – made it very worthwhile. During training, the animals were taught command words, and the weight of people due to be carried was substituted by sandbags.

London — At "The Zoo"

Californian sea lion at London Zoo, c.1903. Surprisingly this pond, which was built in 1864, was originally intended to house porpoises. In fact, sea lions and seals lived here for many years until 1905, when it was engulfed by a large new antelope enclosure. The buildings in the background are the 1861 Antelope House extension and, to the right, the 1876 Lion House.

MARY WITH WALRUSES, ANDY AND 'ARRIET

Walruses at London Zoo, c.1931. A 1931 newspaper cutting about the cost of feeding the animals at London Zoo mentions, 'The two infant walruses lately acquired are starting at £200 a year each [to feed]. If all goes well with them, they will eventually incur a bill of over £1,000 a year in fresh cod, herring roes, mussels, and cod liver oil.'

Seal.—Zoological Gardens.

Seal at London Zoo, postmarked 1905.
This looks like a bull Patagonian sea lion, which was the first species of sea lion to be brought to England alive. After appearing in the circus at Cremorne Gardens, Chelsea, and briefly joining a travelling menagerie, a male arrived at the zoo in 1866.

From the Gardens of the Zoological Society of London, Regent's Park, N.W.

Young Elephant-Seal.

Young elephant seal at London Zoo, 1910s.
A Southern elephant seal was presented by King George V in 1911, but was absent in 1914, when two more arrived as a gift from the Duke of Bedford.

This pool was built especially for elephant seals and was situated immediately behind the Fellows' Tea Pavilion.

LONDON, ZOOLOGICAL GARDENS, ELANDS, ANTELOPES, & SECRETARY BIRD.

Eland and secretary bird at London Zoo, 1900s.
The Antelope House was completed in 1861 and the eland, which had arrived at the zoo in 1851, did very well here – eighty-seven were born between 1853 and 1926.

The secretary bird is a distinctive African bird of prey. Its name is popularly thought to derive from the crest of long, quill-like feathers, lending the bird the appearance of a secretary with quill pens tucked behind their ear. A more recent hypothesis is that 'secretary' is a French corruption of the Arabic 'saqr-et-tair' which means 'hunter-bird'.

Riding the 200 year old Tortoise, The Zoo, London

'Riding the 200-year-old Tortoise. The Zoo, London', postmarked 1927.
A very popular pastime for many years, dozens of photographs exist showing privileged visitors astride the giant tortoises. The ages that these ancient reptiles achieved in captivity was often greatly exaggerated. The Tortoise House was built in 1897, at a cost of £464, beside the 1883 Reptile House (now the Bird House). Walter Rothschild, who founded the Zoological Museum at Tring in Hertfordshire, donated £150 towards it, as well as many tortoises over the following two decades.

First specimen in captivity in the world.

First specimen in captivity in Europe.

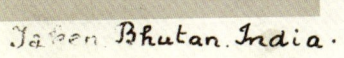

Takin Bhutan. India.

Rocky Mountain Goat. British Columbia.

Takin and Rocky Mountain goat at London Zoo, postmarked 1918.
An unusual card. This male takin arrived in 1909 and was the first living example to reach Europe, and probably the first to live in captivity anywhere. He died in 1918.

The Rocky Mountain goat was purchased in 1900, and was thought to be the first living specimen brought to Europe, as the sender's handwriting claims.

London. "The Zoo."

Bharals at London Zoo, postmarked 1905.
A brief message on the back of this card reads, 'Dear Kate, hope you are well, I am just off to Bible class, goodbye, love from Elsie.' Bharals − or blue sheep − come from the Himalayas, and are uncommon in zoos today.

(5). MAPPIN TERRACES, ZOOLOGICAL GARDENS

The Mappin Terraces at London Zoo, c.1920s. The 'Mappins' were built to house most of the zoo's large collection of wild sheep, goats and bears, and were completed in 1914. They are the largest single construction in the zoo and space was purposely left underneath the 'hills' for an Aquarium to be built. Unfortunately this was delayed by the First World War until 1923. John Newton Mappin, who financed the original construction, owned the firm of Mappin & Webb, a noted silversmith and cutlery manufacturer.

1142   STUDIES AT THE ZOO.   A BROWN BEAR FROM N. RUSSIA PERFORMS ONE OF HER LITTLE TRICKS.

Brown bear at London Zoo, postmarked 1927. 'A brown bear from N. Russia performs one of her little tricks.' It was common for bears to teach themselves a remarkable repertoire of antics to get noticed by the public, in the hope that food would be thrown to them. This bear was called 'Nellie' and she was blind. Nowadays, the public is banned from feeding the animals at London Zoo.

'A close acquaintance with Joan the Hippo at the London Zoo', c.1920s. Keeper Ernie Bowman was frequently photographed in close proximity to the hippos he cared for. The presence of this young child illustrates his confidence with his charges.

THE HIPPOPOTAMUS, LONDON ZOO. (884)

220803.JV.

From the Gardens of the Zoological Society of London, Regent's Park. N.W.

The Thylacine.

Thylacine at London Zoo, pre-1918. The thylacine, also known as the Tasmanian wolf, is now extinct. A total of twenty were exhibited at the zoo between 1850 and 1931. No serious attempt was made to breed from them, despite the knowledge that they were being hunted into oblivion in their native land. The 1906 guidebook states, 'As it does great damage to flocks, it is being killed off by the settlers.'

Entrance to Dublin Zoo, pre-1918. The zoo was opened to the public on Thursday, 1 September 1831. An advertisement in that day's newspaper included this excerpt, 'All persons are to be admitted for sixpence each, and they are to write their names at the gate... The Committee request that visitors leave their sticks and umbrellas at the gate, and that children may be kept from approaching too near to the bars which confine the animals.' This first entrance lodge was built two years later in 1833 and still stands, located to the right of the present entrance.

Entrance to Dublin Zoo.

Entrance to Dublin Zoo, late 1940s. The 1940s saw a phenomenal increase in attendance. During the 1930s, there were about 150,000 visitors per year, but by 1949 that figure was close to 350,000. A similar dramatic increase has taken place in the past ten years – the number of visitors in 2008 was 931,086.

ENTRANCE TO ZOOLOGICAL GARDENS, DUBLIN. R.2134.

Two views of Dublin Zoo, early 1900s. Albert Tower, seen on the right in both of the cards on this page, was built in 1845 to house an elephant, a camel and a giraffe. The foundation stone contained a 'time capsule' in the form of two glass jars containing an illustration of the building, various tickets, newspaper cuttings and a number of metal admission tokens embossed with a giraffe as there was an extra charge for entry to this house. The items were retrieved in 1962, when Albert Tower was demolished to make way for a hippo house.

Two views of Dublin Zoo, early 1900s. The zoo always had many kinds of waterfowl wandering around at liberty. The giraffe glimpsed to the right of this card arrived in 1902, but unfortunately died from pneumonia in February 1904.

Haughton House at Dublin Zoo, postmarked 1905. This was also known as the Haughton Memorial Building to honour the late Dr Samuel Haughton, who was president of the Royal Zoological Society of Ireland for many years. It opened in 1899 and was used as offices and to house monkeys and birds. Every Saturday morning, members of the society meet here to have breakfast and discuss zoo business. At these breakfasts, which take place to this day, porridge is served first and it is a 'quaint unwritten law' that each member must stand during this course!

The lake at Dublin Zoo, c.1900s. The four-acre lake pre-dates the establishment of the zoo, but the island seen in this card was built by the zoo in 1895.

Lion House at Dublin Zoo, postmarked 1911. Built in 1902 by public subscription this house, also known as the Roberts House, was named after Field Marshal Lord Roberts V.C. It still stands today, and is now used for tropical birds.

'Lioness presented by H.M. King Edward VII', **c.1900s.** Dublin zoo was internationally famous for breeding lions. Between 1857 and 1900, two hundred and eleven had been born, although not all of these survived. The first roaring lion that was used as a trademark for Metro Goldwyn Mayer films was born at the zoo in the 1920s.

ZOOLOGICAL GARDENS, DUBLIN.

"JERRY" AND KEEPER.

BOXING KANGAROO   G.E.L.

Lion cub 'Jerry' with keeper Christopher Flood at Dublin Zoo, 1907. Christopher Flood was a popular keeper, who worked at the zoo for fifty-three years until his death in 1933 – he was at work in the Lion House at the time. Christopher started his long career in 1880, shortly after his father, Thomas, had also died at the zoo as a result of an attack by a red deer stag. Christopher's son Charles also worked with the big cats at the zoo for many years.

Boxing kangaroo at Dublin Zoo, postmarked 1916. At this time, 'boxing' kangaroos were frequently featured in travelling shows and circuses, and were a familiar image. This large adult male red kangaroo would have been quite a match!

The Elephant, Zoological Gardens, Dublin.

'The Elephant, Zoological Gardens, Dublin', c.1900s.
This is probably 'Sita', who achieved notoriety in 1903 by killing her keeper, James McNally. Sita was undergoing treatment for an extremely painful foot problem when she unexpectedly knocked McNally to the ground and crushed his head with her foot. The incident was over in about two seconds and, as a matter of zoo policy, Sita was destroyed shortly afterwards.

The Elephant House, Zoological Gardens, Dublin.

Elephant House at Dublin Zoo, c.1900s.
This Elephant House was built in the 1880s to house 'Rama' and 'Sita', a pair of Burmese elephants. A new Elephant House was opened in 1957.

'Elephant House, Zoological Gardens, Dublin', c.1930s.
The Asian elephants seen here could be 'Dingiri Amma', who arrived in 1929, and 'Chancal Peary', who arrived in 1932. Both of these elephants were destroyed shortly after the start of the Second World War. There is a curious gap in the safety barrier where the lady is standing worryingly close to the elephants!

Elephant ride at Dublin Zoo, 1950s. Asian elephant 'Sarawatha' (Sarah) had been having foot trouble for some time when, in July 1958, she tripped and fell while carrying a full load of children. No one was seriously hurt though and she continued to give rides until 1961. Elephant riding was then discontinued at the zoo. Sarah was put down in 1962 after all attempts to cure her foot failed.

The man on the right in the foreground is elephant keeper Jimmy Kenny.

Asian elephants 'Komali' and 'Sarah' at Dublin Zoo, c.1950.
Komali (pronounced 'cummalee'), is the baby Asian elephant in this photograph. She arrived 28 June 1950 when she was about two years old, and lived at the zoo for sixteen years.

GORILLA.   ORANG-OUTANG.
GIBBON.   CHIMPANZEE.

Examples of all four classes of the man-like Apes, photographed by Mr. W. N. Allen, in the Gardens of the Royal Zoological Society of Ireland, during November, 1914.

'Examples of all four classes of the man-like apes, photographed by Mr W.N. Allen, in the gardens of the Royal Zoological Society of Ireland, during November 1914.'
An unusual card, as all of the larger apes represented were difficult to obtain and keep in good health at the time. It was claimed that this was the first time all four types of anthropoid apes had been exhibited together: 'Empress', a young gorilla; her companion, 'Charlie' the chimp; 'Sandy', the orang utan; and, bottom left, is a male hoolock gibbon.

View eastwards across the lake at Dublin Zoo, 1900s. The house shown is the superintendent's residence, which was completed in 1868. When the zoo first opened, the west side of the lake was outside the zoo boundary and unfenced. This caused problems, as people could wade across the shallow parts and enter the zoo for free. Wild deer also swam across and caused damage in the zoo grounds. Eventually, in 1864, the land on the west side was given to the zoo and permission to fence it in was granted.

Restaurant lawn at Dublin Zoo, c.1950s. The Parrot House and the Giraffe House can be seen in the background.

GIBBON ISLAND, DUBLIN ZOO

Gibbon Island at Dublin Zoo, c.1950s. Two gibbon islands were established on the lake in 1953 and 1954. This card also shows the concrete bridge that was built in 1942 to replace a dilapidated wooden one, which dated back to the 1850s. Both bridges were constructed as part of government-subsidised unemployment schemes.

Giraffe House at Dublin Zoo, c.1950s. The first giraffe to arrive was presented in 1844. There were no giraffes at the zoo between 1906 and 1951. In 1955 – approximately when this photograph was taken – the zoo bred the first giraffe to be born in Ireland.

Pony trap at Dublin Zoo, c.1960. The enclosure in the background is the site of the 1832 Bear Pit. When this photograph was taken, it was home to a group of rhesus monkeys, which escaped soon after arriving. They leapt from the small castle turret that had been built especially for them. Nine monkeys even managed to leave the zoo grounds, and were at liberty in the suburbs of Dublin for several days.

In the 1960s, the enclosure was altered again to house chimpanzees, and nowadays it is home to a flock of waldrapp ibises.

Main Walk at Dublin Zoo, c.1950s. The building in the centre is the Elephant House; you can also see the Aviary to the left and the Giraffe House, extreme right.

Longsight Entrance and Hotel at Belle Vue Zoo, c.1900s. The zoo was established in June 1836 and admission was three old pence, for which the visitor also received a non-alcoholic drink and some biscuits!

After one hundred and forty-one years of giving entertainment to millions of people, the zoo closed in September 1977, with the amusement park following in 1980. The land was sold off in 1982 and the site was finally cleared by 1986.

Indian Temple and Grotto at Belle Vue Zoo, c.1910s. Throughout its long history, Belle Vue was always much more than just a collection of animals: within a few decades of opening, it had its own brewery, bakery, dairy herd, gas works, fireworks factory, print works and an electricity-generating plant, among other enterprises. There were always extensive and often very elaborate gardens, rockeries and follies within the grounds. Parts of The Indian Temple and Grotto, which was built in 1870, were still present when Belle Vue closed.

Monkey House at Belle Vue Zoo, c.1910s. Possibly the largest Monkey House in Europe when it was built in 1881, it was designed to look like an Indian Temple. As was the style of the time, it contained a large central cage with a number of smaller cages arranged along the outside walls. The building was heated to a constant 60°F to 70°F, which was, by 1895, considered to be the main cause of ill health among its inhabitants; modifications were later made to provide the monkeys with better ventilation and limited access to the outdoors.

View across the Fireworks Lake at Belle Vue Zoo, c.1910s. Looking east; in the centre is the Indian Rockery and to the right is the Lighthouse Bar. The Lion and Tiger House can also be seen.

Elephant House at Belle Vue Zoo, c.1910s. In 1873, a glass-roofed Elephant House was built to house two elephants, 'Maharajah' and the female 'Sally', who had been acquired in 1872 and 1869 respectively. The original house was superceded in 1875 by an adjoining brick building. The outdoor Elephant Tank – seen on the right – was added in 1906. Most of the major animal houses at Belle Vue were built or modified during the 1870s and 1880s, and went on to serve their various purposes well for the next one hundred years.

Sea Lion and Aquatic Bird House at Belle Vue Zoo, c.1910s. This house was built in 1885 and was sometimes referred to as the Penguin House. At around the time this photograph was taken, it housed black-footed penguins, cormorants and shags, as well as Californian sea lions and a Cape fur seal. A hybrid between the latter two species was born on 4 June 1910 but died shortly afterwards.

Asian elephant in the Elephant Tank at Belle Vue Zoo, c.1906. The keeper is the legendary Lorenzo Lawrence, who famously walked a bull Asian elephant called 'Maharajah' from Edinburgh all the way to Manchester before starting employment at the zoo in 1872. Lorenzo's work at Belle Vue came to an end in 1912, when he broke a leg on a crowded Whit weekend during a momentary panic among two of his elephant charges.

Elephant ride at Belle Vue Zoo, c.1903. This large Asian elephant seems at first glance to be unattended. However, it is quite possible that the man standing to the extreme right is her famous keeper, Lorenzo Lawrence, who was notoriously camera-shy and probably hoped he was out of shot.

THE ELEPHANT RIDE
Zoological Gardens, Belle Vue, Manchester

Belle Vue Gardens.   CONSUL,   Manchester.

Elephant ride at Belle Vue Zoo, c.1949. This is 'Annie', who was purchased at auction in September 1941 for the bargain price of fifty guineas. Elephants at Belle Vue worked for their keep, and in addition to giving rides they were used to move loads around the zoo. Annie was approximately sixty-five years old when she died in July 1952. Her exotically dressed keeper is Phil Fernandez from Malaya, who came to the zoo in 1922 in charge of another elephant called 'Lil'.

Chimpanzee 'Consul' at Belle Vue Zoo, c.1894. Possibly a posthumous postcard as this famous chimp died in 1894. Consul was bought from a travelling menagerie in 1893. He's seen here in a smoking jacket and cap, puffing away on a cob pipe. A larger version of this photograph includes his bottle of beer on a side table!

Polar bears at Belle Vue Zoo, c.1900s. In 1903, C.V.A. Peel wrote a report about the zoo, 'The polar bears form a beautiful picture in their light-built cage under a knoll covered with noble forest trees that dip their roots in the shady waters of the lake.'

Behind this cage and also built into the 'knoll' were two bear pits; a climbing platform can just be seen to the left beneath the trees.

Brown bear at Belle Vue Zoo, c.1920s. The 1847 guidebook mentions just one bear at Belle Vue; others were added, and to begin with they were kept beneath the Natural History Museum, near the main entrance. Bear pits and the polar bear cage were constructed between 1853 and 1855. They remained in use until July 1960, and were finally obliterated in early 1964 when the new lion and tiger enclosures were built.

Giraffe at Belle Vue Zoo, c.1910s. The first giraffes arrived at Belle Vue in 1871, when four were purchased. A small Giraffe House was built in 1878, but all the giraffes died and the house was dismantled in the early 1880s. For a while, the zoo gave up trying to keep giraffes.

Giraffe at Belle Vue Zoo, c.1905. The zoo was without giraffes until a male of the Kordofan subspecies was added to the collection in 1905. As the Giraffe House had been demolished decades earlier, he was exhibited in the 1881 Camel House across from the Paddock and had an adjacent outdoor enclosure.

Flamingos at Belle Vue Zoo, c.1900. These look as if they might have been housed somewhere in the Indian Grotto. At some point before 1903 they were moved to an extensive open-air enclosure.

Bactrian camel and calf at Belle Vue Zoo, c.1900s. Newborn Bactrian camels have two dark-coloured folds of skin on their backs which gradually fill with fat as they grow. The youngster in the photograph looks about five to six weeks old and was most likely born at the zoo. Camels at Belle Vue used to share their accommodation with giraffes, when they were obtainable, and many other species including zebus, gnus and tapirs.

Entrance to Zoological Gardens, Clifton

The Downs Entrance to Bristol Zoo, early 1900s. In 1902, the admission to the zoo was six old pence, and it was open to the public from 9am to sunset on weekdays. On Sundays, only shareholders and subscribers were admitted, and the zoo closed at 4pm. It was eventually opened to all and sundry on Sundays in 1924.

The zoo changed from being popularly known as the Clifton Zoo to the Bristol Zoo sometime in the 1930s.

THE ZOOLOGICAL GARDENS, CLIFTON, BRISTOL

BR 116

The Downs Entrance to Bristol Zoo, postmarked 1951. The zoo, which opened on 11 July 1836 is the fifth-oldest in the world. It is also often described as the oldest 'provincial' zoo. Bristol's size has never expanded: it occupies just 12 acres of what was formerly farmed downland on the edge of Clifton, a suburb of the city. The world-famous Clifton suspension bridge is nearby.

179. "Kruger" & His Keeper, Clifton Zoo.

Boa Constrictor, Born in the Clifton Zoo. 1901. 1453.

Boa-Constrictors and **Pythons** belong to a family of the innocuous Snakes (Colubriforms) known as Rock Snakes. To compensate for the deficiency of poison glands these reptiles have tremendous crushing powers. Pythons are the largest of all snakes, some specimens measuring 30 feet in length, with a circumference as large as that of a man's body.

Chimpanzee 'Kruger' and his keeper at Bristol Zoo, early 1900s. Up to 1928, Bristol had only kept juvenile chimps in inadequate cages in the Parrot House. However, in 1928, the Large Mammal House near the entrance was converted into an Ape House. It was here, in 1934, that Bristol became the first zoo in Europe to breed a chimpanzee.

'Boa constrictor born in the Clifton Zoo, 1901', late 1900s. This was quite an achievement at the time as, unlike today, breeding was not a priority at most zoos. Boas are not particularly difficult to breed these days; one advantage is that – unlike most snakes – they bear live young, which eliminates the difficulties associated with incubating eggs.

Kiwi, chimpanzee and cockatoo at Bristol Zoo, pre-1918.
Kiwis are very seldom exhibited in zoos nowadays, partly
because they are extremely shy and strictly nocturnal – the
exact opposite could be said of chimpanzees and cockatoos!

Bear Pole at Bristol Zoo, c.1900s. There was a bear pit in use
at Bristol for more than one hundred and twenty years. One of
the many bear poles from this long history can still be seen
today at the entrance to the Aquarium.

CLIFTON ZOOLOGICAL GARDENS, THE AVENUE.

The Avenue at Bristol Zoo, c.1900s. Better known as the Great Terrace, The Avenue was part of the original landscaping by Richard Forrest of Acton, London. It was said at the time, 'A noble terrace of five hundred feet in length already offers to the delicate and infirm, the infant and aged, a dry sheltered and sunny walk.'

THE TERRACE & NEW LION HOUSE. ZOOLOGICAL GARDENS, CLIFTON.

'The Terrace and New Lion House. Bristol Zoo', postmarked 1912. The 'new' Lion House was built to the west of the original Lion and Tiger House in 1900. It became an Ape House in 1928, and was home to Bristol's famous gorilla 'Alfred' for many years.

Polar bear enclosure at Bristol Zoo, c.1900s.
This enclosure was more commonly called the Polar Bears' Court. It was built against the eastern side of the Elephant House, where the Pygmy Hippo House is today. It was occupied by polar bears until 1935.

Refreshment Pavilion at Bristol Zoo, c.1915.
To the left is the 1836 Bear Pit and its outside cages, which were constructed in 1907. When the zoo grounds were first purchased in 1835, it was intended that they should be laid out not only as zoological gardens but also as an arboretum, and the zoo still has many fine ornamental trees.

Entrance to the Parrot and Reptile House at Bristol Zoo, c.1900s. This building, which is virtually in the centre of the zoo, was constructed in 1892 and is still standing today.

Interior of the Parrot House at Bristol Zoo, c.1915. At this time the zoo's reptile collection was located behind the parrots, within the same building. In 1951, the reptiles were relocated to a house of their own, built on the site of the old Monkey House.

The Eagle Aviary at Bristol Zoo, c.1900s.

This card reads, 'I am writing this with a new fountain pen I bought... we were at this place yesterday, we saw these birds. I hope you are all quite well, with love from all to all.' This aviary was a feature of the zoo for more than one hundred and twenty years, and was finally demolished in 1962.

Zebras at Bristol Zoo, postmarked 1907.

The man with the whip is elephant keeper Jim Rawlings. At this time, zebras and camels were also accommodated in the Elephant House.

Monkeys with keeper at Bristol Zoo, c.1915.
All of the monkey houses in the UK's principal zoos were built along similar lines at this time, with a large central cage – sometimes divided into two or three compartments – and smaller cages ranged against the outer walls. These houses were usually unnecessarily overheated and badly ventilated, and monkeys did not do well in them.

Monkey Temple at Bristol Zoo, postmarked 1928.
The Monkey Temple was first opened in 1928 and still stands today. This photograph was probably taken on, or close, to the opening day.

Mascot monkey at Bristol Zoo, c.1915. 'Cigarette fund for my Regiment. I have been many months with the troops in France. Had a toe shot away and was gassed at Neuve Chapelle and invalided home. Please give me pennies to send out cigarettes. Signed Jack.' Tobacco and cigarettes were greatly appreciated by the men in the trenches. Nationwide charitable funds were set up from the outset of the First World War.

'Durbar elephant, now at the Clifton Zoo', 1913.
This is 'Rajah', newly arrived from Calcutta Zoo. As seen in this photograph, he had a fine pair of tusks. Visiting children chose his name by majority vote, and he was housed in the 1873 Elephant and Giraffe House, which is still in use today as accommodation for gorillas and the giraffe's nearest relative, the okapi.

Asian elephant 'Rajah' at Bristol Zoo, c.1915. Rajah was used as a riding animal for many years, although it was quite unusual for male elephants to be trained for this task as they generally have unpredictable tempers.

Asian elephant 'Rajah' at Bristol Zoo, 1910s. Rajah lived at the zoo for thirteen years. In 1926, he was sold to a French collection, but unfortunately died on the day he was due to leave Bristol.

Asian elephant 'Zebi' at Bristol Zoo with keeper Jim Rawlings, 1900s. Zebi was presented to the zoo in 1868 by the Maharajah of Mysore, and died in January 1910.

Asian elephant 'Zebi' in the bath at Bristol Zoo, with keeper Jim Rawlings, 1900s. Zebi was said to be one of the largest of her species in captivity and was a great favourite with the public, who admired her independent spirit.

ALFRED THE GORILLA AT THE BRISTOL ZOO.

Gorilla 'Alfred' at Bristol Zoo with keeper Frank Guise, c.1930. Alfred was two to three years old and weighed twenty-five pounds when he was purchased for £350 on 5 September, 1930. He was hand-reared in the Cameroons and was extremely tame and friendly, arriving at the zoo (from Rotterdam, via several animal dealers) on a collar and chain. At the time, Alfred was the only gorilla in the country. For the first two years, he was allowed to take walks around the zoo and could make and throw snowballs with accuracy!

AT THE BRISTOL ZOO 98 GORILLA. "ALFRED." JULY. 1938

'At the Bristol Zoo. Gorilla 'Alfred'. July 1938.' Alfred became famous worldwide and was a popular attraction for almost eighteen years. It was recorded that in one year during the Second World War, 20,000 postcards of him were sold. He died on 10 March, 1948, and his skin was mounted by the most famous firm of taxidermists in the UK, Rowland Ward of London. Today, Alfred can be seen at the Bristol City Museum & Art Gallery.

In the late 1930s, keeper Frank Guise (seen through the bars) was attacked by a chimpanzee and retired on health grounds soon after.

COPYRIGHT
BL. 165

ZOOLOGICAL GARDENS, CLIFTON, BRISTOL.

Lion's cage at Bristol Zoo, postmarked 1937. In 1905, outside cages were added to the Lion and Tiger House, and the whole layout of the house was altered. At about the time this photograph was taken, the zoo had a large collection of big cats, including at least six lions, 'several' tigers, leopards (including a black panther), pumas and cheetahs.

"AT THE BRISTOL ZOO" 99 TIGER AND LIONESS BORN IN THE GARDENS. JUNE. 1937

'At the Bristol Zoo. Tiger and lioness born in the gardens. June 1937.' The original Lion and Tiger House was built shortly after the zoo opened. The floors of the indoor cages were made of teak, and the big cats thrived and bred frequently in this house.

Giraffes at Bristol Zoo, c.1930s. This pair of giraffes 'Alphonse' and 'La-La' produced three calves during the 1930s, but the first of these didn't survive beyond two days. Unfortunately, the adult animals also died before the end of the war.

This subspecies, known as the Rothschild's or Baringo giraffe, is now considered to be critically endangered.

Okapis at Bristol Zoo, c.1964. Okapis are related to giraffes, and were unknown to science before 1901. In 1963, Bristol Zoo became the first UK collection to breed them; however, the calf lived only a few months. The first to be reared successfully was born in 1966.

Asian elephant 'Rosie' at Bristol Zoo, c.1950s. Rosie was purchased in 1938 and quickly became a great favourite with visitors. She was estimated to have given more than 80,000 rides during her time in Bristol. The zoo stopped elephant and camel riding in the late 1950s, and Rosie died in 1961.

Camel riding at Bristol Zoo, c.1950s. The Arabian camels used for riding during the 1950s came from Somaliland in August 1947, and were bred by Bishareen arabs.

Brown bear 'Rosie' at Rosherville Gardens, c.1903. This zoo was originally called the Kent Zoological and Botanical Gardens. It is documented as opening in 1837 but then closing in 1900, after years of decline. However, in 1903 the gardens were re-opened by a group of local businessmen. A small menagerie was acquired which included a baby elephant called 'Kim'. Rosie must have been installed at about this time. Despite the best efforts of the various managers, Rosherville Gardens was still not a success and they finally closed in 1913.

Blackpool Tower Menagerie, c.1902.

Opened in May 1894, the Tower replaced Dr William Cocker's Aquarium, Aviary & Menagerie, which had opened about twenty years earlier on the same site. The new developers bought Dr Cocker's animals, tanks and cages for £4,000. The menagerie was built into the first floor, to the left of the foyer, and the Aquarium was installed directly underneath on the ground floor. After almost eighty years of operation the menagerie closed in 1973, but the aquarium, modernised over the years, is still there to this day.

THE TOWER MENAGERIE AND MONKEY HOUSES

Blackpool Tower Menagerie, c.1900s.

This postcard was issued in slightly different versions for many years, which was perfectly valid as the scene depicted remained unchanged for most of its long life.

Four Tiger Cubs, Born in the Blackpool Tower Menagerie, June 29th, 1907.

REARED BY COLLIE AND AIREDALE FOSTER-MOTHERS.

'Four tiger cubs, born in the Blackpool Tower Menagerie, June 29th, 1907. Reared by collie and Airedale foster-mothers.' The menagerie had a good reputation for breeding big cats including lions, tigers, jaguars and pumas. One tigress successfully reared twenty-four cubs in twelve years.

Lions at Blackpool Tower Menagerie, postmarked 1913. The big cats were mostly kept in a range of twelve cages built along the north wall of the main hall. In 1907, it was reported that the menagerie exhibited 'eleven lions, five tigers, three leopards, five jaguars, an ocelot and two small domestic dogs of a hairless breed'.

LIONS TOWER MENAGERIE BLACKPOOL.   660

'Chimpanzees tea party, Blackpool Tower Menagerie', postmarked 1956. The chimpanzees usually lived in the largest cage, which was tiled from floor to ceiling and had a large bowed window facing south-west. As the window could also be opened, the chimps not only enjoyed a view of the Promenade but could also sample the bracing Blackpool sea air.

CHIMPANZEES TEA PARTY, BLACKPOOL TOWER MENAGERIE

Blackpool Tower Aquarium, c.1902. The fake rockwork was inspired by the famous limestone caverns of Derbyshire. It would have been quite innovative at the time this photograph was taken.

THE TOWER AQUARIUM, BLACKPOOL.

Children's Corner at Southport Zoo Park. Photo by W. Simpson Cross, postmarked 1908.
Southport has had a number of zoos over the years. This one opened c.1906.

An interesting postcard as the sender was the zoo's director, William Cross himself and the intended recipient R.I. Pocock, the superintendent at London Zoo. The back of this card reads, 'Menagerie L'pool, 18/2/08. Dear sir, I have now one pair slender & one pair slow loris if these would be of interest to you. Yours truly, W. Cross.' Pocock was superintendent at London zoo from 1903 to 1923.

Bactrian camel at Southport Zoological Park. Photo by W. Simpson Cross, postmarked 1907.
Another card sent by Cross himself, 'Menagerie L'pool 9/4/07. W. Cross begs to state that he does not supply sand for parrots.'

All of the animals depicted on these two postcards perished in a fire on 22 October 1908. Cross left the zoo at about the same time and it seems to have closed at the beginning of the First World War.

Alexandra Palace Monkey House and Zoological Collection, early 1900s. Two intriguing cards, as they appear to be two photographs of the same doorway, taken at about the same time, but the entry sign in each of them changes dramatically and someone has also added (or removed) a statue to the right of the pay desk.

Alexandra Palace Monkey House and Zoological Collection, early 1900s. The man wearing a hat is Captain Henry, who previously worked for the famous circus entrepeneur 'Lord' George Sanger. He appears in other contemporary postcards taken at Alexandra Palace which show a jumbled collection that includes live animals such as baboons, cockatoos and bear cubs alongside glass cases filled with mounted animals.

Entrance to Zoo. Stoke-Under-Ham, c.1903.
This ramshackle zoo at what is now known as Stoke-sub-Hamdon in Somerset looks truly depressing, and it's a good thing that it is now long forgotten and consigned to the past.

Siberian wolves at the zoo, Stoke-Under-Ham, c.1903, postmarked 1906.
The back of this card reads, 'Have just been in the zoo – thought you would be glad to know we were not kept there as specimens. Love from Elsie.'

It's a great pity that anything was ever kept as a specimen at this zoo. Hopefully the wolves seen here were tame enough to be let out once in a while.

HALIFAX ZOO. AND AMUSEMENT PARK.

Halifax Zoo and Amusement Park, c.1909. This zoo opened 29 May 1909 at Chevinedge, Exley, just south of the centre of Halifax. As well as animals, the zoo boasted many other attractions. One of these was the cinema, then referred to as the 'Electric Theatre'. It was said to be the first of its kind outside London, although there had already been something similar at Belle Vue. The large house is Chevinedge Mansion, which housed the zoo's tea rooms.

THE ELEPHANT.

HALIFAX ZOO. AND AMUSEMENT PARK.

Asian elephant 'Nigger' at Halifax Zoo and Amusement Park, c.1909. Seventeen-year-old Nigger was at the zoo when it opened, having had a former life at the Scottish Zoo and Variety Circus at Glasgow, where she was known as 'Kim'. Nigger must have been a valuable addition to the park as she was used to give rides during the summer months.

'The Teddy Bears' Parade' at Halifax Zoo and Amusement Park, c.1909. Quite a number of bears were kept, including 'Jack' and 'Jill', who were described as 'Rocky Mountain bears'. The dimensions of these cages seem very small, even for the time, and were probably dictated by the single panel of bars that each cage incorporated, which very likely came from a travelling beast wagon. Two bears escaped on 17 June 1913, and one of these made its way out of the zoo grounds before being recaptured, after spending two hours at liberty in nearby Elland Wood.

Lions at Halifax Zoo and Amusement Park, c.1909. Lions bred at the zoo and this pair, 'Wallace' and 'Alice', were probably the parents. Many of the animal houses and cages at Halifax appear to have been built using bricks that were either glazed or painted white. The bars on this enclosure look as if they have been recycled – probably from a circus beast wagon – as they are helpfully labelled '1', '2', '3' and 'Front' (although someone has purposefully taken the trouble to scratch over them on the card).

HALIFAX ZOO, AND AMUSEMENT PARK.

Dwarf Brahmin bull at Halifax Zoo and Amusement Park, c.1909. Among the many attractions at Halifax was a 'Pygmy Farm', which housed dwarf forms of cattle, sheep and pigs. Brahmin cattle come from India and are considered sacred in Hindu society.

THE ZEBRA.

HALIFAX ZOO, AND AMUSEMENT PARK.

Zebra at Halifax Zoo and Amusement Park, c.1909. A contemporary article in *Animal Life* by C.V.A. Peel states: 'Zebras have often been broken to harness; here in England, Mr Walter Rothschild used to drive a team of these animals. Burchell's zebra costs from a hundred to a hundred and fifty pounds.'

The zebra in this photograph looks like a Chapman's zebra, a subspecies that is very similar to Burchell's and one that was readily available at the time.

HALIFAX ZOO, AND AMUSEMENT PARK.

Zeedonk at Halifax Zoo and Amusement Park, c.1909. Hybrids − such as this one between a zebra and a donkey − have been bred for research purposes, or simply as objects of curiosity for more than two hundred years. The earliest recorded zebra hybrid was between a male donkey and a female mountain zebra, bred by Lord Clive in 1773. Extraordinarily, it was decided to paint stripes on the donkey to aid its acceptance by the zebra!

A VIEW IN THE ZOO AND AMUSEMENT PARK.−HALIFAX.

Yak at Halifax Zoo, c.1909. The message on the back of this card is direct and to the point, 'To sister Mary, from Dick with best love, 1 August 1910.' This curious-looking animal might not be a pure-bred yak.

Monkey House at Halifax Zoo and Amusement Park, c.1909. The back of this card reads, 'I am sending you a PC of the zoo, this is one of the monkey house, we went in and we did enjoy it...'

HALIFAX ZOO, AND AMUSEMENT PARK.

Halifax Zoo.

HALIFAX ZOO

Halifax Zoo, c.1909. During the First World War, it became evident that the zoo was losing its popularity. It was also becoming increasingly difficult to obtain food for the animals. In 1916, the animals were sold, and the last advertisement for any attraction was in 1917. The mansion was demolished in 1933 and houses were eventually built on the site. This is an attractive card, with a finely detailed embossed mount effect.

Zebu at Mr G. Tyrwhitt-Drake's Private Menagerie, Cobtree Manor, Maidstone, 1912. In 1912, Garrard Tyrwhitt-Drake was elected to Maidstone Borough Council and began a lifetime of public service. He first opened his private zoo to the public in 1910. According to the caption, this bull, along with his 'native' attendant, won first prize at the 1912 Maidstone Street Pageant.

No. 5   ZEBU OR SACRED INDIAN BULL WITH NATIVE ATTENDANT, 1st PRIZE MAIDSTONE STREET PAGEANT, 1912,
AT MR. G. TYRWHITT-DRAKE'S PRIVATE MENAGERIE, MAIDSTONE.

'Maidstone Zoological Gardens, Tovil Court, Yellow Baboon, West Africa', 1914. Garrard Tyrwhitt-Drake's second attempt at operating a public zoo was at Tovil Court, Maidstone. It lasted just a few months, and closed in October 1914.

Although these two photographs appear to be of the same baboon in the same corner of its cage, the view beyond the bars changes. Was this animal in transit? An intriguing card.

Maidstone Zoological Gardens, Tovil Court, Yellow Baboon, West Africa.

'Maidstone Zoological Gardens, Tovil Court, male Indian leopard 'Tom'', 1914. Tovil Court occupied about 15 acres and was situated just a few miles from Cobtree Manor, which continued to be opened sporadically on Wednesday afternoons only until 1917. Wednesdays were chosen because this was the early-closing day for shops in Maidstone.

Maidstone Zoological Gardens, Tovil Court. Male Indian Leopard "Tom."

Maidstone Zoo Park.
FEMALE INDIAN ELEPHANTS, " Gert " & " Dais," with Mr. G. Tyrwhitt-Drake.

'Maidstone Zoo Park. Female Indian elephants 'Gert' and 'Dais', with Mr G. Tyrwhitt-Drake', May, 1936. This pair of elephants arrived at the zoo in May 1936 and were 'christened' at the zoo by their namesakes Elsie and Doris Waters, who were a radio and stage variety double-act, best known for their comic songs and sketches, and for their Cockney characters 'Gert' and 'Daisy'. A double-tier cake was part of the ceremony; the top part was for the elephants, the lower tier was sold in aid of charity.

Lady Edna Tyrwhitt-Drake with lion cubs at Maidstone Zoo Park, c.1930s. Miss Edna Mary Vine married Garrard Tyrwhitt-Drake in 1925. Her Ladyship title was bestowed in June 1936, when Garrard was knighted 'for public services'. Cobtree Manor had opened as a full-time zoo two years earlier in March 1934.

Lions bred prolifically at Maidstone Zoo and were Sir Garrard's favourite animals.

The Polar Bears, Maidstone Zoo Park.

Polar bears 'Sam' and 'Barbara' at Maidstone Zoo Park, c.1955. Sir Garrard believed that the most dangerous animal in captivity was the polar bear. Speaking about all bears in general, he stated that, 'The mentality of a bear is a quaint mixture of buffoonery and spitefulness. They have enormous strength, are amazingly quick and well equipped with teeth and huge claws... they cannot be bluffed and kept at bay, and they seem impervious to pain when in a temper.'

The Lion Terrace, Maidstone Zoo Park, c.1955.

The Lion Terrace, Maidstone Zoo Park, c.1955. These two enclosures were built in 1937. The surrounding fence was 14 feet high, with an overhang. Sir Garrard thought that this should be enough to contain the lions, but commented that if his beliefs were wrong, 'lion shooting in Kent will soon be in season!'

Sir Garrard always believed that lions were happier housed in circus-style beast wagons because wooden flooring was warmer and more comfortable than concrete. Also, being off the ground, they were relatively free from draughts.

ARK. 2.   BISON

American bison at Maidstone Zoo Park, c.1950s. The keeper, who joined the zoo in 1932, was known as 'Captain' Gates. He lived on the estate for many years, even after the zoo's closure in 1959 and Sir Garrard's death in 1964.

Californian sea lions and Egyptian goose at Edinburgh Zoo, c.1934.
In 1930, two Egyptian geese left their own paddock and moved in with the sea lions. The gander refused to be returned, and lived alone with the sea lions for many years. This enclosure, which was formed from natural rock in 1914, is one hundred feet by approximately sixty feet, with a depth of more than six feet. It has been home to sea lions, that have often bred here, for almost one hundred years.

SCOTTISH ZOOLOGICAL PARK, CORSTORPHINE, MIDLOTHIAN.   THE BEAR POOL.

Brown and polar bears at Edinburgh Zoo, c.1913.
The back of this card reads, 'Dear Francis, We saw them drive the bears from this big place into their cages for the night. The white bear was so frightened it took 20 minutes to coax him out. Then we saw them fed. The white polar bear fed raw meat: about 10 pounds. The brown bears eat bread.' These three bears, 'Daisy', 'Baby' and 'Snowball', were purchased from the Marine Gardens at Portobello, Edinburgh. They were among the first animals acquired for the zoo, and had to be housed temporarily in the garden of an empty suburban house while the zoo was being built.

Bactrian camel at Edinburgh Zoo, c.1934.
Edinburgh Zoo was opened to the public on 22 July 1913, and was incorporated by Royal Charter later that year. It is the only zoo with a Royal Charter in the United Kingdom.

Following a visit by King George VI in 1948, the Zoological Society of Scotland was granted permission to add the prefix 'Royal' to its name.

Asian elephant at Edinburgh Zoo, postmarked 1934.
This is 'Sundra', who was about four years old when she arrived in 1914. She lived at the zoo for almost 30 years.

Lion at Paignton Zoo, postmarked 1935. Originally called Torbay Zoological Gardens, this was millionaire Herbert Whitley's large private collection. It first opened to the public in 1923, only to close the following year because Whitley refused to collect entertainment tax. He was of the opinion that a zoo was primarily a place for education and not 'amusement'. Eventually he relented and re-opened his zoo in 1927, only to close it again in 1937!

Tiger at Paignton Zoo, c.1930. In 1930, the zoo changed its name to Primley Zoological Gardens and produced its first guidebook. Two more name changes followed, with it finally settling on Paignton Zoo and Botanical Gardens in 1946.

Multiview card from Paignton Zoo, postmarked 1948. The lion, top left, was named 'David', and was considered to be one of the finest in the country. Beneath David is one of the alligators that Herbert Whitley had raised from hatchlings; they lived in what was the best Tropical House in the UK at the time. Whitley designed this house himself, allegedly using the backs of old envelopes to scribble ideas for the layout. It was completed in 1934.

The young llama, seen here with his mother, was born in March 1947.

Multiview card from Paignton Zoo, c.1950. The chimpanzee was called 'Charlie', the young Asian elephant was one of a pair imported from Bangkok in 1949, while the leopard, 'Prince', was one of a pair that arrived at the zoo in 1948.

Sun bear at Grimsby Zoo, c.1930s. This small zoo, which lasted about a dozen years, was situated at the end of College Street in Grimsby. It closed in 1939.

Common seals at Grimsby Zoo, c.1930s. Admission to the zoo cost sixpence and, in addition to seals and bears, there were lions, an Arabian camel, monkeys, the usual assortment of parrots, peafowl and so on, as well as a Reptiliary and a small Aquarium.

Fallow deer at Whipsnade Zoo, c.1952. The old farmhouse at Whipsnade was converted into a restaurant. It was enlarged in 1935 and windows were added that overlooked Home Paddock, which housed fallow deer and a variety of waterfowl. This photograph epitomises Whipsnade with its peaceful sense of space and quiet. The area shown is now used for a free-flying birds display.

Ostrich Enclosure
Whipsnade Zoo

White rheas at Whipsnade Zoo, 1930s. When the estate was bought in 1929 it was little more than a run-down farm. Many miles of roads and paths were laid, and thousands of trees were planted. The first guidebook stated, 'In future, as the necessary funds can be found, the light fences enclosing the paddocks will be replaced by deep ditches, so that there will be no barrier between the eyes of the visitors and the animals'.

The white rheas shared their paddock with llamas and, despite the caption to this card, ostriches were housed elsewhere.

THE ZEBRAS' CREATE INTEREST, ZOOLOGICAL PARK, WHIPSNADE

'The Zebras create interest. Zoological Park, Whipsnade', 1930s. This is Spicer's Field, the largest enclosure at the zoo. During the early years, it housed zebras, ostriches, cranes and, during the summer months only, pygmy hippopotamuses.

BACTRIAN CAMEL RIDING, WHIPSNADE PARK

'Bactrian camel riding, Whipsnade Park', c.1930s. In 1936, Whipsnade began to build up a herd of Bactrian camels by importing one male and three females direct from Russia. The first calf was born in 1937, and soon the zoo owned the only breeding group in the UK. The policy was to sell only males – valuable to other zoos as riding animals – and to keep the females to ensure the zoo's monopoly.

Old & Young enjoy the Elephant Ride at the New Zoological Park. Whipsnade

Elephant ride at Whipsnade Zoo, early 1930s. This is most likely to be 'Nur Jahr', who was at the zoo when it opened. It took her a while to settle in: it was said that she was particularly unnerved by the peacocks that were at liberty around the zoo if they 'suddenly expanded and elevated their trains before her'. Hall Farm restaurant can be seen in the background.

WAITING FOR AN ELEPHANT RIDE, ZOOLOGICAL PARK, WHIPSNADE

'Waiting for an elephant ride. Zoological Park, Whipsnade', 1930s. There were a total of five Asian elephants kept at Whipsnade prior to the Second World War, but only two – 'Nur Jahr' and 'Dixie' – were used as riding animals. Nur Jahr, who came from London Zoo, was notorious for not allowing anyone to ride on her neck. Twenty-nine-year-old Dixie was purchased at the sale of Bostock & Wombwell's menagerie in Glasgow in 1931. She lived at the zoo until her death in 1963.

The Bear Pen, Whipsnade Zoo, c.1930s. This original enclosure is still in use today. When it was first constructed in 1930, it represented a revolutionary new way to keep bears, allowing them more space with natural vegetation and a large bathing pool. In 1931, an old female bear from the London Zoo named 'Mary' surprised her keepers by producing and successfully rearing cubs.

Sloth bears at Whipsnade Zoo, c.1934. In its early years, Whipsnade kept brown, Himalayan black, sloth and polar bears.

Camel Paddock, Whipsnade Zoo.

Dromedary at Whipsnade Zoo, c.1930s. A 1930s zoo guidebook explains what a dromedary is: 'Selective breeding has given rise to two main types of Arabian camel: the baggage camel, capable of carrying heavy loads for days at a steady pace of two or three miles an hour; and a more lightly built riding or racing camel, capable of carrying a rider at eight to ten miles an hour for hours on end. The name dromedary rightly belongs only to this latter type.'

Bison on the Hillside. The Zoological Park. Whipsnade

'Bison on the Hillside, Whipsnade Zoological Park', c.1930s. The American bison enclosure was vast, with a circumference of about a mile. Ironically, when the bison were first introduced they rarely strayed far from the shelter, which was situated in one corner.

Whipsnade originally planned to build a lake at the bottom of Bison Hill; this never happened, but another large enclosure did house Barbary sheep for a time.

'Greeting the Public, Whipsnade Zoo', c.1940s. Asian elephants in the Elephant House. This house, which was listed Grade II in 1988, was designed by modernist architect Berthold Lubetkin as a Tecton group project and completed in 1935. It is made of reinforced concrete, lined with heat-insulating panels of cork. The 1936 guidebook stated, 'There is a bathing pond between the visitors and the elephants, just wide enough to allow the elephants to stretch across with their trunks to take food from the outstretched hands of visitors.'

GIANT PANDA, WHIPSNADE

Giant panda at Whipsnade Zoo, early 1940s. Three giant pandas, 'Sung', 'Tang' and 'Ming' arrived at Whipsnade from London Zoo during 1939, and were kept in a pen just north of the Elephant House. By May 1940, only the youngest, Ming, was still alive. She travelled back and forth between London and Whipsnade, enjoying celebrity status and helping boost morale throughout the war years. Ming died at London Zoo in late December 1944.

Main Drive at Chester Zoo.

Main Drive at Chester Zoo, c.1950s. The zoo opened in June 1931, and consisted of just nine acres set around Oakfield House. Admission cost one shilling for adults and sixpence for children. By the time this photograph was taken, the zoo had expanded to more than seventy acres. Today, Chester has a world-class zoo that covers one hundred and ten acres.

Emu and Wallaby Enclosure. CHESTER ZOO.

Emu and Wallaby Enclosure at Chester Zoo, c.1950s. This enclosure, which had an Australian theme – despite the inclusion of a small flock of Soay sheep – was very near the North Entrance and adjacent to the Aquarium.

'Approaching the Polar Bear Enclosure at Chester Zoo', 1950s. The polar bear enclosure opened 21 June 1950. By the end of that decade Chester already had a reputation for providing its animals with some of the finest accommodation in Europe, particularly for lions, chimpanzees and bears. This enclosure was famously made from redundant wartime cement road blocks and pill boxes.

'View of the Breeding Aviaries at Chester Zoo', c.1950s. The struggling zoo received a major boost in 1934 when a collection of four hundred tropical birds were presented – and their future upkeep guaranteed – by Miss Esther Holt. The Holt family, which ran a shipping company on Merseyside, was extremely supportive of the zoo and donated many other animals, including mandrills and chimpanzees from West Africa.

Molly and Barbar with their Mahout at Chester Zoo.

The Black Bear looks hopefully for tit-bits at Chester Zoo.

Asian elephants at Chester Zoo, c.1951. Nine-year-old 'Molly' and another younger elephant arrived with their keeper at the end of 1941, after the start of war had interrupted a travelling show and stranded them in Britain. Their keeper (or mahout) was Khanadas Karunadasa, better known as 'Kay'. As a ten-year-old, he had trained Molly in Ceylon and the two were inseparable. This photograph was taken in the zoo's first custom-built Elephant House, which was completed in 1948. 'Barbar' arrived in 1949, having been at both London and Whipsnade zoos for the previous twelve years. She died in 1972.

'The black bear looks hopefully for tit-bits at Chester Zoo', c.1951. Bears have always been a feature at Chester. Two Canadian black bears 'Adam' and 'Eve' were among the first few animals at the zoo when it opened in 1931. By 1938, the zoo had added Himalayan, polar, Russian brown and Malayan bears to the collection. The enclosure shown in this photograph was completed in 1945. In 1962, the zoo kept twenty-five bears including a breeding pair of enormous Kamchatka brown bears. Today, the zoo specialises in spectacled bears, a species classified as 'vulnerable' in the wild.

Boating Trips on the Canals at Chester Zoo.   ZCR·10·

Motorboat at Chester Zoo, c.1950s. In 1947, this part of the zoo was featureless until a system of lakes and waterways were constructed. By 1959, the zoo had organised a motorboat trip, which took visitors along about a mile of waterways, passing zebras, antelopes, bison and other cattle before returning to a landing on the main lake.

Interior of the Zebra House at Chester Zoo.   ZCR·40·

Zebra House at Chester Zoo, early 1950s. This house and the area around it were a part of the rapid post-war expansion – using war surplus materials – that the zoo enjoyed in the early 1950s. It still stands today.

ARABIAN CAMEL   OXFORD ZOOLOGICAL GARDENS

Arabian camel at Oxford Zoological Gardens, c.1932. This zoo, which opened 4 July 1931, was formerly a farm with substantial outbuildings. After just six years the zoo closed and the majority of the stock was transferred to Dudley Zoo, which opened in May 1937.

The Arabian camel in this photograph was named 'Black Boy'.

SACRED BABOONS   OXFORD ZOOLOGICAL GARDENS

Sacred baboons at Oxford Zoological Gardens, c.1932. They bred at the zoo in December 1931. The baboons shared a large outbuilding with fifteen other simian species. These included mandrill, drill, yellow baboon, Hanuman langur, rhesus and bonnet macaques, brown and weeper capuchins, sooty mangabey, patas, grivet and mona monkeys.

Sacred (or Hamadryas) baboons come from Ethiopia and south-west Arabia. Their former range extended into Egypt, where they were sacred to the Ancient Egyptian god Thoth.

Bonnet macaque at Oxford Zoological Gardens, c.1932. These monkeys come from southern India and are an uncommon sight in zoos today. Modern legislation would certainly not allow the public to get as close as this.

American bison at Oxford Zoological Gardens, c.1932. The bison enclosure was situated in what used to be the farmyard, and was flanked by swamp deer to the east and nilgai to the west.

POLAR BEARS   OXFORD ZOOLOGICAL GARDENS

Polar bears 'Frankie' and 'Johnny' at Oxford Zoological Gardens, c.1932. These arrived at the zoo as cubs in August 1931. Polar bears are great zoo favourites and this pair entertained thousands of visitors both here and later at Dudley (page 113).

TIGRESS   OXFORD ZOOLOGICAL GARDENS

Tigress at Oxford Zoological Gardens, c.1932. Tigers lived alongside the polar bears in the Lion House, and bred at the zoo on at least one occasion.

Oxford Zoo had a good collection of carnivores which, in September 1932, included three species of bears, lions, pumas, hyenas, wolves, jackals, foxes, badgers, raccoons, coatis, kinkajous, civets and mongooses.

Chessington Zoo from the air, c.1950s. The Surrey
Zoological Gardens opened 26 July 1931, but had changed
its name to Chessington Zoo and Circus within just a few
years. The circus, clearly seen in this photograph, moved
to this location in 1936 after a fire had destroyed the big
tent, with the loss of five ponies and a zebra.

"JOHNNIE" DIRECTING TRAFFIC
SURREY'S ZOOLOGICAL GARDENS, CHESSINGTON

**'Johnnie directing traffic, Surrey's Zoological Gardens,
Chessington', c.1930s.** Johnnie is a young drill, a large
baboon-like monkey from equatorial Africa. In early 1932,
two young drills 'Johnnie' and 'Percy' escaped and were
at liberty for two days before being recaptured.

CHESSINGTON ZOO FROM THE AIR

BEARS' TEA PARTY. SURREY'S ZOOLOGICAL GARDENS CHESSINGTON

'Bears' Tea Party, Surrey's Zoological Gardens, Chessington', c.1939.
These 'shows' took place three times a day during the summer; the last performance was as late as 8.30pm, and the zoo closed at 9.30pm.

In 1938, a female brown and a male Himalayan black bear produced two cubs which could be the pair on the left of this card. They resemble brown bears, but one has a distinctive white chevron on its chest – a characteristic of the Himalayan black.

This is a relaxed scene, even though the bears are quite large and would be more than a handful if they decided to misbehave!

AUSTRALIAN BROWN KANGAROOS—"RANG & RENEE" SURREY'S ZOOLOGICAL GARDENS CHESSINGTON

'Australian brown kangaroos – 'Rang' and 'Renee', Surrey's Zoological Gardens, Chessington', c.1939.
Kangaroos are reported as arriving in 1937 and breeding the following year. Chessington successfully bred a lot of its stock during the late 1930s including wallabies, leopards, tigers, lions, llamas and black-footed penguins.

It is unusual to describe this species as 'brown' as they are normally called red kangaroos.

YOUNG INDIAN ELEPHANT—" ROSIE," SURREY'S ZOOLOGICAL GARDENS, CHESSINGTON

'Young Indian elephant 'Rosie', Surrey's Zoological Gardens, Chessington', c.1930s. Rosie came from Chipperfield's Circus and arrived in February 1932. The zoo operated a circus in its grounds from 1934, and Rosie was billed as taking part in an act called 'The Barber's Shop'.

LLAMA RIDES, SURREY'S ZOOLOGICAL GARDENS. CHESSINGTON

'Llama rides, Surrey's Zoological Gardens, Chessington', c.1930s. An early guidebook reminds visitors that 'the llama has an unpleasant habit, if annoyed, of spitting into the face of the person who has incurred its displeasure'. This succinct reminder could explain why llamas have seldom been used as saddle animals.

The mansion 'Burnt Stub', which is at the heart of the zoo, can be seen in the background.

CHESSINGTON ZOO

Pets' Corner at Chessington Zoo, postmarked 1950.
The entrance to Pets' Corner was beside the distinctive domed aviary seen in this photograph. The zoo had many similar cages scattered throughout its grounds. This one was used for rhesus monkeys during the 1950s.

PELICAN "HAPPY" WITH FLAMINGOES   SURREY'S ZOOLOGICAL GARDENS, CHESSINGTON

'Pelican 'Happy' with Flamingoes, Surrey's Zoological Gardens, Chessington', c.1930s.
Pelicans usually enjoy long lives in captivity, so Happy could have been the unfortunate bird that a 1950s guidebook reported as having an accident that necessitated the amputation of a portion of its wing. After convalescing, the pelican was returned to its pond, where it settled down happily. Large birds such as flamingos and pelicans are always pinioned when they are kept in an unroofed enclosure, so this poor bird seems to have been particularly unlucky.

LYNX (CANADIAN) AT LIVERPOOL ZOOLOGICAL PARK

Canadian lynxes at Liverpool Zoological Park, c.1932. This was the third zoo to be established in Liverpool. It was in operation from 1932 to 1938. The Canadian lynx is considerably smaller than its Eurasian counterpart at approximately half the size.

Billy the Yorkshire 'mug' and his midget racehorse 'Tishy' at Liverpool Zoo, postmarked 1936. Perhaps more interesting than Billy and his steed is the inset photograph, showing the entrance to the zoo which was on Elmswood Road. Visible just inside the entrance are the zoo offices and Elmswood café, (formerly known as Rosemont café).

Asian elephant 'Simla' at Liverpool Zoological Park, 1932. Simla was more than thirty years old when he arrived at Liverpool, having travelled the world with various circuses and menageries. He was housed in a centuries-old castle at the zoo. Simla died in November 1932.

"SIMLA" AT LIVERPOOL ZOOLOGICAL PARK.

A pair of lions 'Rex' and 'Dora' at Liverpool Zoological Park, 1930s. The young man sharing the cage is probably a circus lion tamer who obviously knows the animals very well.

"Rex and Dora"   Liverpool Zoo Park.

"Mickey lights up"   Liverpool Zoo Park.

Chimpanzee 'Mickey' lights up at the Liverpool Zoo Park, 1930s.
Mickey was quite a celebrity at the zoo and enjoyed a considerable amount of liberty; he is seen here with zoo manager Mr Wardle. Unfortunately in 1938 he became uncontrollable, and after severely biting several people he was shot dead.

" BILLIE "—PELICAN AT LIVERPOOL ZOOLOGICAL PARK

Pelican 'Billie' at Liverpool Zoological Park, c.1932.
Billie was housed with cranes in an enclosure west of the monkey cage.

OUTDOOR MONKEY CAGE AT LIVERPOOL ZOOLOGICAL PARK

Outdoor monkey cage at the Liverpool Zoological Park, c.1932. The zoo also operated as animal dealers and had a large quarantine station within its grounds. In 1938 three hundred rhesus monkeys were imported; these were probably destined for other zoos, the pet trade and medical research.

YOUNG OSTRICH AT LIVERPOOL ZOOLOGICAL PARK

Emus at Liverpool Zoological Park, c.1932. Wrongly captioned as young ostriches. Emus thrive in zoos and breed freely. The male bird usually does all the work: after gathering together the newly laid eggs, he takes sole responsibility for incubating them. The earliest recorded successful breeding was at London Zoo's farm at Kingston, Surrey, in 1830.

"ROSIE"—NYLGAHI ANTELOPE AT LIVERPOOL ZOOLOGICAL PARK

'Rosie', a nilgai, at the Liverpool Zoological Park, c.1932. Nilgai are the largest of the Asian antelope species from northern India and eastern Pakistan. Females have a yellow-brown coat. Males' coats gradually darken to a slate-blue as they reach maturity. 'Nilgai' is Hindi for 'blue bull'.

In 1929, George Jennison of Belle Vue Zoo wrote, 'The earliest importations cost almost as much as elephants, but now they are so cheap, hardy, easily housed and fed that few zoological gardens are without them.'

BROWN BEARS—"TEDDY & GOBO" AT LIVERPOOL ZOOLOGICAL PARK

Bears 'Teddy' and 'Gobo' at Liverpool Zoological Park, c.1932. This pair were imported from Canada. They are most likely to be black bears, not brown bears, as stated in the card's caption. They were housed next door to the Canadian lynxes.

Multiview of Dudley Zoo, c.1940s. Dudley Zoo opened in May 1937 in the grounds of Dudley Castle. The building of an entire zoo from scratch was not undertaken lightly. A new material, reinforced concrete, was used extensively. Twelve of the thirteen original structures designed by the Tecton group of architects survive to this day, and are Grade II-listed. The missing one is the original Penguin Pool, bottom left on this card, which was demolished in 1979.

Aviary and Monkey Enclosure at Dudley Zoo, c.1950s. This is a view looking west, and is typical of the wooded, hilly terrain of most of the zoo's forty-eight acres. At the time this photograph was taken, the aviaries – seen on the right – were used to house pheasants, jungle fowl, doves and budgerigars.

MONKEY ENCLOSURE AT DUDLEY ZOO

Monkey Enclosure at Dudley Zoo, c.1950s. This was home to a large group of Hamadryas and Guinea baboons, and rhesus monkeys. In 1938, a large iron wheel four foot in diameter was set up in the enclosure, but it was only enjoyed by the monkeys; the baboons regarded it with 'lofty contempt'.

POLAR BEAR PIT AT DUDLEY ZOO

Polar Bear Pit at Dudley Zoo, c.1950s. The bears came from Oxford Zoo when it closed, and were called 'Frankie' and 'Johnny' (see page 101). They were trained for eighteen months to learn to jump into their pool from the top of the diving stand; however, they only performed the trick at feeding time.

Lion Pit at Dudley Zoo, c.1950s. The Lion, Tiger and Polar Bear Pits were fashioned from limestone quarry workings. Large quantities of rock were blasted out and concrete walls added to prevent the animals from jumping out.

LION PIT AT DUDLEY ZOO   80788

Lion Pit at Dudley Zoo, c.1950s. The concrete slabs that the lions are resting on were fixed at different heights so that the public could see the cats from different vantage points, even if they were sheltering from the bad weather.

LIONS AT DUDLEY ZOO   80772

SEA LIONS AT DUDLEY ZOO

80784

'Sea lions at Dudley Zoo', c.1950s.
In 1938, the zoo installed 'twopence-in-the-slot machines' which allowed visitors to buy pieces of fish to feed the sea lions between 2pm and 7pm. *Animal & Zoo* magazine reported: 'When the sea lions rush to obtain the food, the keepers have to watch the big bull, Georgie, carefully lest he gets even more than the (sea) lion's share of food.'

DUDLEY ZOO, FLAMINGO ENCLOSURE & CASTLE RESTAURANT

80773

Flamingo Enclosure and Castle Restaurant at Dudley Zoo, c.1950s.
Both the Sea Lion Pool and the Flamingo Enclosure were made from reinforced concrete and built into the shape of the castle moat.

Bear Ravine at Dudley Zoo, postmarked 1939. The Bear Ravine was described at the time as 'a very large reinforced concrete amphitheatre, supported on columns of novel construction, that gives an unobstructed view for large crowds'. The lower tier was also used for the ubiquitous chimpanzees' tea party. Brown, American black and Himalayan bears were kept here when the zoo first opened.

Brown bears at Dudley Zoo, c.1950s. A close-up of a section of the Bear Ravine, which was said to be the largest bear enclosure in the country when the zoo opened.

THE ZOO PARK, WELLINGBOROUGH

'The Zoo Park, Wellingborough', c.1950s.
The three-and-a-half-acre zoo was situated in the gardens of 12th-century Croyland Abbey. It was opened to the public on 12 June 1943. Swanspool Brook, home to various waterfowl, can be seen in the foreground. The zebra enclosure is to the left. Wellingborough Zoo closed in 1970 and the area is now the Borough Council Offices and Swansgate Shopping Centre.

Wellingborough Zoo Park, view of Extension.
Opened by George Cansdale of TV.

'Wellingborough Zoo Park, view of Extension opened by George Cansdale of TV', 1950s.
George Cansdale was superintendent at London Zoo from 1948 to 1953, and was a well-known television personality. He opened the extension at Wellingborough in 1954. According to a contemporary report, it accommodated 'peafowl (including white peacocks), a llama enclosure and other animals'. It was accessed by a bridge over Swanspool Brook.

At Wellingborough Zoo Park. "Blondie" Polar Bear, Christened by:- George Cansdale of TV.

'At Wellingborough Zoo Park. 'Blondie' polar bear, christened by George Cansdale of TV', 1950s. George Cansdale continued his zoo-related career throughout the 1950s, 1960s and 1970s. He founded Sandown Zoo on the Isle of Wight, and was also a director of Morecambe's Marine Land, Chessington Zoo and Natureland in Skegness.

Polar Bears at Wellingborough Zoo Park.

Polar bears at Wellingborough Zoo, c.1940s. Despite the small scale of this zoo, it always maintained a large collection of familiar animals such as camels, chimpanzees, lions, tigers, leopards, penguins, zebras, deer, sea lions and orang utans. There was even a young elephant here during the 1960s. Somehow the zoo also managed to fit in a Reptile House, Model Farmyard, Pets' Corner, Children's Play Area, Tea Canteen and what was called Rabbit Village!

'Lawns & Paddling Pool, Wellingborough Zoo Park', 1950s. By the time this photograph was taken, the zoo had increased in size to seven and a half acres. Any further expansion would have been difficult, as the zoo was situated in the very centre of the town.

Lawns & Paddling Pool, Wellingborough Zoo Park.

Chimps 'Penny' and 'Chicko' at Wellingborough Zoo, postmarked 1967. The faint, curved lines are a not very successful attempt by the card's manufacturer to remove the long lead that each chimp is wearing to prevent them from running amok. It would be at least another two decades before 'PhotoShop' was even thought of!

Penny and Chicko,
The Chimps at Wellingborough Zoo Park.